© 2018 by Dawn Renee Blanchard. All rights reserved.
Published by Vantage Point Publishing
Indianapolis, IN 46205

No part of this publication may be reproduced or transmitted in any form or by any means, electronic or mechanical, including photocopy, or any information storage and retrieval system, without permission from the publisher. The only exception is a brief quotation in printed reviews.

Limit of Liability/Disclaimer of Warranty: While the publisher and author have used their best efforts in preparing this book, they make no representations or warranties with respect to the accuracy or completeness of the contents of this book and specifically disclaim any implied warranties of merchantability or facilities for a particular purpose. No warranty may be created or extended by any persons. The advice or strategies herein may not be suitable for your situation. You should consult with a professional where appropriate. Neither the publisher nor author should be liable for any loss of profit or any other incidental damages, including but not limited to special, consequential, or other damages.

This is a work of fiction. Names, characters, businesses, places, events and incidents are either the products of the author's imagination or used in a fictitious manner. Any resemblance to actual persons, living or dead, or actual events is purely coincidental.

ISBN 978-1-943159-10-9

LCCN 2018908692

The publisher would appreciate notification where errors occur so that they may be corrected in subsequent printing and/or editions. Please send comments to the publisher by emailing to

deeprivers67@yahoo.com

Printed in the United States of America

Cover Photo by Kay Joe Unscripted

Unscriptedforreal@gmail.com

Cover design by

Gerald Johnson Jr.

Grjcustoms@gmail.com

Dedication page

I dedicate this book to my family and all that believe in who I am.

My beautiful children that are always there. You are all grown now but Anthony, Domonique, Aundreas and Adrian you are still my babies. I never want to imagine life without you.

To those special people that know who they are that would not let me not publish this book. I focus on everyone else and their work I tend to forget mine. Thank you for the push.

To my partners in all this literary jungle that we call life, Steven words are never going to be enough, and Gerald as you know you are stuck with me. We are in this until the air is no more.

To my parents, my gifts are because of you!!
Love Always
Dawn Renee

A gift of poetry!

Ink Drops

by

Dawn Renee

The sun rises around the darkness that I live in

The air smothering as I fight to breathe

Heat sweltering….body swelling with no relief in sight

Words that leap from my heart and continue to fall in the valley

Lost with no one there to catch them

Emotions that swim in the rivers

A race to the finish of nowhere

Tried to fight

But who really wins a fight when you are blinded

By the mere obstacles that stand in your way

Hearing escapes you

As you continue to see with your ears

And listen with your eyes

While your eyes are blind

And ears deaf to all that is reality

You cease to get out of your way

Struggling with the man/woman in the mirror

Trying to pay for air that is free

And the struggle right before your eyes

That even a blind man could see

We have to remember even with closed eyes

To always enjoy the sunrise…..

Many ask....

If you could go back....

and talk to anyone from the past...

Who would it be?

Simple answer to a complicated question...for some

My answer came with no hesitation....

To sit at the feet of my ancestors...

Listening closely.....

Holding my breath...

At times, many times I am at awe..

With the stories that I know will be told...

The descriptive words that create vivid pictures..

As the wind whispers softly in the background..

Giving a melody to the stories that I know will be told....

I see off in the distance...

What is...what was....

The history of who I am...

The legacy that so many never want us to have...

Made to feel less than...

When my soul pleads with my spirit....

To let me know that I am Royalty...

Nothing less....

The trials and tribulations that they went through.....

So that I could be....

Just to know the stories of where I come from....

To know that the stories are our history...

A legacy built on the backs of many....

I want to sit at the feet of my ancestors...

To know where I came from....

So that I will understand....where I am to go....deep rivers

My soul is not your playground....
and my spirit is not meant to be broken.....
with the atrocities that you insist on draping me in....
my heart has been mutilated....
extracted.....
and replaced with a mechanical repetitious.....
on off switch.....
the warmth...cold....dark and stripped....
my love....captured....held hostage.....
as what remains. ..needs to be rejuvenated....
with hope and faith.....
as my mind shattered into pieces of the words....
that are needed to start again.....
a heart the size of the universe....
treated like outdated memories ...
with no change in sight....
my soul is not your playground.....
grown folks play in the real world.....
not fairy tell land......
I'm done.....running on empty......
so I'm going nowhere fast....
Love has cost me everything....
my reward. ...
nothing....deep rivers

My heart dances to the darkness
which allows the soul its freedom
flying free to a blank canvas
Kiss me until I say stop
Pampered by each kiss you give
no need to rush the moment
the beauty in taking it slow
If he only knew the truth
truth that releases both of us
Trust starts within then with others
Very true from start to finish
And everyone believes in their truth
Many die that should never die
While others live that should die
Never underestimate my complex creative mind
Truth the sincerity of my depth
A force that soothes with words
Closed eyes that see with clarity
while ears hear what's not said
Understand before you try to advise
The book more than a cover
Understand my words and their story….deep rivers

Spirits that meet with the beat of an African drum....
the rhythm in sync with two beating hearts.....
that understand the silence.....
that tells the story....
with eyes that screams to be free...
along the shore of knowing...
Mentally sacrificing the soul....
committed to the satisfaction of it all....
the wrapping of two souls into one.....
the entity...
that as one receives all the pleasure of the heart....
splashes of color....
that continue to dance in the melody of freedom....
no limits...no wants....
as the silence screams....
the passion and the love created.....
strokes that give life to a masterpiece.....deep rivers

My heart dances to the darkness

Which allows my soul to embrace freedom freely

Steps that flow to a melody that is created anonymously

A masterpiece that comes naturally

Strokes that intertwine with a rhythm that allows me

To dance with each key stroke

The creation of my rhythm and blues

As I take flight

To fly free to a blank canvas

Colors so vivid that jump from the canvas of life

As your heart dances to the darkness

Stripped of all negativity

Painted with positivity

Breathe in and taste the flavor of freedom

Exhale the smile that shows that you are

A breath of fresh air

To dance in the darkness….my calm reality…..deep rivers

The blanket that has covered me from me
Allowing the sun to shine and life to flourish
Winds blowing
Lightning strikes across that sky
And the heart that wants to capture the trust
Foundation that seems to be built
On the top of the volcano that explodes
Whatever sits in the depths of the core?
When explosion occurs
Left to build all over again
Floating above the clouds
Tears that rain down on the foundation
Of whom she never knew
A tortured soul that wants more than release
She searches for peace
The love that has been raped from the shine in her eyes
She walks with her mirror image
Of whom she wishes she knew
Callouses that continue to cover the wounds of who she is
The mirror image that we all see and wish we could be....deep rivers

Transformed by the very thing that gave her life
Left to stand before the clouds
Left to stand through the storms
Left to fight a battle all alone
Left to go right in a battle that has now become hers
The shell that cracked like a dozen of unwanted eggs
Spirit lifted then tossed in the river of unknown
See so many never see pass the surface
The hurt hides like the thief in the night
Never wanting to be found
Afraid of that which is bigger than they
Or that which can't be explained
The moon and the stars
The water that runs up stream never wanting to run down
The blues that plays
And we all smile and sing along
Right to go left
Or left to find what's right
This thing called poetry that I run from at times
As a sleepless mind needs to rest
And the words fight sleep as they cry out
To be heard
The hurt hidden by the shell that smiles
The tears that only the clouds see
Broken beyond understanding

And so many only see strength
The facade of an abandoned soul….deep rivers

She was bullied…..
And no one thought to correct the problem
She killed herself soon after
He was teased, didn't look like the others
And the trick played
He never learned to swim
So he breathes no more
He wanted to get his praise on
But his friends laughed
And he sat in the back and never made a sound
She wanted to dance
Girl, that ain't possible as big as you are
And she kept eating, no one was the wiser
She loved him and he laughed at her
All he wanted was her money and to use her car
And she let him for the moment to be seen with him
The days go by and no one stops to see the hurt that is inflicted on
so many
Walking through a world that mistreats, abuses and discards it
very own
And we say the land of the free
Free from what
Land of whose
This is not what any of that means
We are at times the worse of the worse

Trying to teach those to love themselves when
Those that live right in the same house tear them down
The mirror image has to change or we will not survive
Do you like what stares back at you…..deep rivers

I sit and see

Hear and read

Tragedy and turmoil

Sickness and death

That continues to plague so many

Left right up down

All around

With no change in sight

No relief

More black dresses sad singing and flower bringing

And the mothers that try to heal a wounded heart

Close the empty hole

That has taken the place of a smile

The sound of laughter

That shines in their eyes

And all we here is the screeching sound of rescue vehicles

That rescues no one

It's too late

Dammit it's too late and then

More and more

Mothers dropping to their knees

Screaming why me Lord why me

And then it happens all over again

When is enough, enough

When will the children get to see laughter?

And rid of the tears
Constant loss
Is common when life should be
Violence has become the commonality
The reality
That continuously destroys
As the cycle running faster than the child can run
When will this all be done?
Tears that flow forever…with hope and a prayer for
peace…..deep rivers

Kiss the dark side of love

As it ventures across the rainbow of nowhere

Emotions that seem to amount to the stack of empty dreams

That never seems to reveal them

Building hope and laughing as it comes crashing to the ground

Absorption no more

The hurt and disgust sits

In the belly of the beast

Sun fighting with the moon for a place in the atmosphere

Or will this be another shining day or the darkness that continues

in the

Hell who knows

Words that sometime make absolutely no sense at all

But the fight to be heard

Taking a stand to be seen

And my mind does the only thing it can

I close my eyes and type

And hope for the best

Or at least my spelling follows something that I have learned

along the way

The reality of it all

The surge of release that exploded inside me

Is …..

How do you feel such loneliness in a room full of friends…deep

rivers

My addiction and paternity crossed the uncommon lines
Connected not because they want to be but they crossed and became my humility
See what was is now and the lines crossed and stretched around my neck and pow!!!
The wind knocked clearly out of me
Or did it do more?
Stripped from who I thought I was into what I don't know
I feel lost
Steps taken in a nightmare that seems to never end
Glass beneath my feet
As each step is so damn tricky
How many paths to turn down
It is not as easy as go left or right
I know that it should be
I tell so many that the gift of life is more than anything else
But I sit and know she gave me life but at this point she can't get anything else
No recognition….as I feel you gave me life and then set out to destroy me
Step by step you sat and laughed at me
Belittled all that I was and even now I still feel the grip of your hand
Around my neck, squeezing what life I have left out of me
Falling slowing into the pit of hell

You gave me my addiction because of your hatred of not what I did

It was what you did…..and could not face your own demons

Set out on the path of my destruction because of your malfunctions

I have forgiven but I can't lie that it creeps back in to haunt me

And it probably will for the rest of my life

Every time I look in the mirror…..as ask myself who are you?

And no, I can't answer my own question…..and you can't answer for me

I don't know who I am…..and neither do you….hell you don't know who you are

I guess we share the same demise

As we both have hidden behind this happy disguise

And I know God has carried me through it all

I am human and God knows my call and the fall

That I battle with….

See my addiction was caused by my paternity

The trickle down effect of your actions not mine

My image the day to day sign……

Who am I….deep rivers

A heart is on over load….

Leary not secure in anything

As the tears fall my mind listens

As I am the only one that hears

The despair written in plain view

But hidden

Heartache

The loneliness you have when standing in a room full of best friend strangers

Lost in a whirlwind of darkness

I breathe in and out and

My hear hurts, physically playing jump rope inside

Suffocation and I reach for the lifeline

And it was broken at birth

The reasons that I cannot

Explain as you took that away from me

Walked away leaving me with more questions than answers

I am so tired

Tired

And if you only knew

My last breath is the one of peace

As for now I live in constant misery…consumed with so much that my mountain top is turned upside down

And my waterfall is dry…no sun on the dark eyes of the river….deep rivers

Loyalty turns into soiled sheets

While royalty hides secrets behind concrete….attorneys and walls

Life sentence with no chance of parole

No love lost as the only real want

Never crosses the minds of the ones who matter most

That would not be

The lack of reality or the disdain for fantasy

All the track has ran out and the only option

Is to be released

Let free

Sentenced complete

Not that there is gold at the end of this rainbow

Last time I checked just another storm

Waiting to pick up where this one left off

Ain't no sunshine when she's gone

Hell last she checked the sun packed up and moved away

Leaving her to stay

In the darkness

With no chance of rain

As we have moved into a new season

The thunderstorm replaced with a winter storm

Hot and wet into cold and dry

And all I want to do is smile and kiss the sky

Giving an inch of hope to survive…..deep rivers

Is our history a fairy tale that they want us to believe?
Or is the truth to harsh so we walk on cotton sidewalks of comfort
Letting someone dictate
Not even the slightest chance to relate
To what reality is
Walking with heads held high
No need to drop to your knees and wish for
The history is there to consume you
If only we picked up a book
And most of the truth lies between the pages of banned books
Banned because the truth usually hurts the ones that don't want us
to know
Never allow someone to tell you your history
When you should be educating yourself on who you are
The royalty blood line that bleeds for us
Kings and Queens that produced a heritage that is so rich
That are streets should be made of gold
And we continue to disrespect what cannot be changed
History that is filled with greatness
It has been said many times before
And right now it needs to be in the forefront of everyone's mind
The truth shall set you free
To know who you are, will allow you to know the path of where
you are going
To not know, only leads you in circles….deep rivers

Fast running feet that are going nowhere...

Mouth moving…..

With a taste of not saying enough.....

Or too much and still not getting anything done....

Spinning in circles with no out...

I don't want to play this game.....

My heart is dizzy and my mind has officially reached overload....

My love needs to be felt...

Not lost across the ocean....

Floating in midair....

Not even feeling the coolness of the water...

And I am slowly melting into nothing....

Fast feet running nowhere....

But plenty of places I need to be...

And going at the pace of standing still…

Directions that read like a foreign language…

And it's not the one that I took…..

Nowhere does it read this way in my handbook….

And then I realize that this chapter as yet to be written….

Stuck waiting for the ink to spill…..

Once again I stand still…..

deep rivers

The dark secret

The unseen

Hidden but in plain view

Dragged down

Stripped

And tossed about like salad

That no one wants

Sleep hardly ever comes to visit

And some days the energy has you running around

Everyone asking what is she on

If they only knew

Walk a day in my shoes

I think not as most would never survive

Seeing the smile on one's face

Without knowing that the tears

Fight to stay back

While the muscles are going a few rounds

That absolutely no one wins

Stuck on repeat of

This doctor

That doctor

Those doctors

That in the end some had you marked as crazy

Well hell if you felt like I did

Suffering daily

You would feel crazy too

But my crazy is the strong want

Desire

Need

Please

To have some relief

Just because you can't see my pain

Believe me it is real

Usually at 3-4 a.m. it lets me know it still there

Auto immune disease, you will not win

Fibromyalgia, I don't have time

I have been blessed with many gifts

So that means I have lots to do

And that doesn't leave time for you

I got things to do….deep rivers

A tortured soul

Lost without no direction

The voice silenced

My pen has no ink

No hope for the weary eyes

That search for a life line

Help to see what has been done to me

To get pass the pain

Told time and time again to get over it

Leave it in the past

But how when no apologies were ever given

And never will
To calm the heartache that no one sees
You took from me what I demand back
My life….deep rivers

I have ventured down so many ragged roads
Life has drifted to so many illusions
When my mind wanted what was not there
Slipped in the mirage of what can be
See the moments that continue to exist
In the depth of the rivers
Fight to reach the surface of waters
That no one even knows
My presence seen but so misunderstood
Lost on the thought of
Eternity
Words that come and go like the wind
While my spirit floats along the dock of the bay
Or am I drowning in my own grief
As if I know
I just breathe
And allow what will to be….deep rivers

Beauty stopped at my door
Whispered the song of greatness in my ear
So many never know what I know
The beauty of what lies within
The heart that loves all
The eyes that glisten when graced with your presence
The hands that feel the security when wrapped in
The lips that place soft kisses on wounds the size of the world
And they heal them
Ears that listen to screams of pain and silence of all that smiles
Two feet that will walk a million miles to say a simple, Hello
Beauty is so much more than the surface
It goes to the depths of what we cannot see but what we feel
Heat that shines
With a cool breeze that sings a melody
Beauty is in all of us
The design of perfection in imperfection
Beauty is…..deep rivers

The song went something like "Home of the Brave"
But all I continue to see
Is constant killing of the innocent by cowards
Mother's burying their children around the clock
While the system sits back and clocks the dollars that are made
With the prison system steadily being filled
The image of fear that has replaced the smiles of the innocent
Trapped inside behind close doors that still won't stop a bullet
That has no name
It destroys whatever it hits
And then we are left with parents throwing fits
Because once again they have to bury a child
Most folks scared to go outside
Stay inside
Or hide
And it seems that it's still in plain view
Of the bullet that has no eyes
Let alone a name
Killed for what reason
Just because the season
Changed or remains the same
The rhyme or reason
Makes absolutely no since at all
No solution given as more bullets are driven
Into the lives of the innocent

And I pray for the one's that drop the tears for their loved ones
"Home of the Brave" as the song goes "land of the free"
Then why do we feel in captivity……deep rivers

The sound of your voice

No words spoken

The arousing scent that feeds my soul

Wet lips that taste your aroma

As you come close to desire

Beating of anticipation

Heat of waiting gratification

As my needs build for rejuvenation

From a touch that warms

A caress that sends chills

The length of my spine

And then a kiss that brings thunder and lightning to my soul

Give me as I give in return

Sharing the thirst of each other

As we quench together as one......deep rivers

They say when your mind goes one way
And your body is craving so much more
You need to be heard
The cries are so strong
I don't understand the transformation
That is taking place before my eyes
The beast that has been released
To prey upon what needs to be fed
My deepest desires
And nothing less will do
I am
So I will be
Even when you think
Less of me
I know my strength
The silence that kills
The touch that will melt you before my eyes
The kiss that will have you begging for forgiveness and you have
done
Nothing
I am and this I know
I will not change my stripes
I cannot go back
I am the creation that will
Be

We sit and wait
The movie plays out and you didn't understand the plot
You didn't follow the script
You tried to rewrite it to fit your need
But failed because of your greed
You think out of sight out of mind
That would be to kind
And that is just not in my dna
I play hard but fight even harder
Laced in black garter
Locked and loaded
Protecting mine from beginning to end
You really have no clue this battle you will not win
The darkness before the light
The love before the fight
The bullet that comes like a thief in the night
Warnings that will come no more
Love stopped at the door
And fell drastically to the floor
Weep at forgiveness door
The story that has been told may times before
And now my silence all that's left
No more tears
No more pleas of what should be
Darkness has replaced all that was light

As now you are left to fear the wrath that comes in the night
You will only know but by then it will be too late
No one to blame
Your mouth determined your fate
Time never taken to evaluate
Nothing left but hate….deep rivers

As I walk the path of discernment
I realize that my shadow walks with me
My shadow is always there in darkness and light
The darkness seems greater when my mind went left instead of right
And dimmed the light that rested at the end of the tunnel
The light that I constantly reach for
It seems to knock at my door and when opened
All that stands is darkness
The mistakes that are made
That continues to reside without forgiveness
Are the weights that hold my shadow down?
I know my shadow is forever with me
But for once I want it to shine
Forgiven for what has been done
But also to forgive thyself
Set free from what was so that I can walk in what is…..means this
"Accepting that a misunderstanding does not make a shadow
The people who you hurt from the misunderstanding
And what they decide to say or do about it
Is what leaves a shadow
The only way to erase that shadow is to shed light on it….and hopefully they will forgive you"
Once all is done the light shall shine…..deep rivers

Sitting here waiting

Contemplating

Devastating

Recuperating

And yes I still

Sit in silence

The explosion that is about to take place

The doubt

No one ever really believed

That no matter

Her brain is always on scatter

They didn't think that I would be

Pass the fantasies

I am reality

Words that speak more than the letters ever will

Stretched across the rivers that wash them away

And they still reappear

My words dig deep

Slice and dice the average reader

Because the surface was left a long time ago

I had to reach as far as the sun would allow me

And then travel to the darkest side of town

Before I would

Could

Shall

And I still know that I don't know how
But it is
The blessings that flow with no reason
And so many walk backwards instead of to them
I wait
Contemplate what is next
Arms wide open as I received all that is for me
Words raped time and time again
Now they heal one at a time
To be stronger than they ever were before….deep rivers

Open wounds

Tears that flow

Stabbed deep in the back of nowhere

As the shots ring off in the distance

Open wounds that never seem to heal

Open wounds that we all pay the price for

Stretched out on the stretcher of open wounds

The crime that not just one pays

The crimes that the village pays

The price more tears that flood the ever after

Over charged over and over again

As the lessons learned the first time not enough

And open wounds continue to stay gaped open

For the salt to season all over again

Deaf ears are the only ones that seem to listen

Until the interpreter pays a visit to yet another open wound

When will the wound have chance to heal

As the constant anger

Grows with each day

Growing while the child never gets the chance to

The constant let's do, what never gets done

The ghost of yesterday's past continue to keep it going

To lose the battle that pours once again into open wounds

Left with the fear of

The want to

Where do

We start

Or is it

Too late

To save

What is

To be

Our future….deep rivers

Trapped in my own mind

drowning in my own river

suffocating on the air that no longer fills my lungs

scattered thoughts and no one reads between the lines

emotions that float to the clouds and get washed away

with the tear drops that rain upon me

words raped from the moment the letters appear in my mind

as they float to paper with no chance of survival

taking back all that has been stripped

when will the pain ease

wanting the soft caress

the kiss that says more than words can

but the pain prevents what is needed

running away to what my shadow brings along

not a chance in the sky

to realize that the air is no longer

the savior for many that now suffers in silence

and the heart continues to ramble

lost

forgotten

never to be again

and the words continue to invade my thoughts

so many battles fought

tired time to lay it to rest

the battle won

the war has begun

and not many will understand

as they think no further then themselves

dreams that never awake from the nightmare

that holds them hostage

battered in a mirage of what ifs...

I watched him from afar
Inhaled his words
Deep as they dwell in my mind
As I held on to each words that his lips
Released….
Wanting to explore him
Learn what made him tick
To understand what drove him
What is his passion?
Words that describe his being
Tall caramel blended with hazel nut crunch
Eyes that pierce the soul
With confidence and a splash of humility
Rolled into that which captured my soul
Words that leave his lips
And I catch each one and savor
Sensuous and seductive flavor
What my heart longs for
As he has not a clue
The things that he does
The emotions that have risen from captivity
Only to hide in the darkness
Afraid of rejection because I am not his type
Shy to the reality that I dream about
Wish upon a star

And simply wonder what he would do
If only he knew
Fantasizing about the touch that his strong hands give
With a soft caress that melts
Causing the rivers to release
The imagination to flow
But he has not a clue
As I sit and wonder what could be if only he saw in me
What I see in him
Unconditional.......deep rivers

I scream in silence

I whisper in volumes that no one hears

Is it that no one cares?

The same story different day

The reality that my soul darkens

While my spirit hovers in a loss place

So my body is frozen still

I ask over and over again

If he only knew what his words do

The presence of him

The warmth that rises in the mist of my thoughts

I looked pass the eyes deep into his soul

And the strength that he possessed rose high up from the valley

To the mountain tops and the light blinded my soul

I knew then that he was the one

The soul mate that completed a puzzle that only pieces of life fulfill

The magic that that was missing the link to make troubles disappear

Yes he is that

And the crime committed the sentence given

The cell that holds me

Captive in my own thoughts

Hurting inside

Trapped from the outside

Suffocating on the air

That he breathes

And then once again I whisper

If only he knew what his words create

His lips vibrate

And I sit here in a stalemate with my thoughts

If only he knew….

If he could see in me what I see in him…..

Affirmation…..deep rivers

My silence is not for you to misuse

Tired of being your toy and it's nowhere near Christmas time

And Santa never impressed me

To see the constant mind games

The games that so many play and now I am part of

The not now, maybe later, we shall see game

What the hell happen to a balance in life?

The soul that was stripped from me

Your words ripped my sanity from my grasp

As I fell solemnly to nowhere

I am not a toy

Strength that produces life

Something you will never understand

Without the spread of my hips

The gentle lips

That separate and give life

Yes I am

And I also finally reached that point

Who the hell cares about me?

The pain that I continuously go through

But give the smile of a champion

While my insides explode into pieces that cannot

Will not be put back together

I am tired

The string has been stretched and it has no more elasticity

My creativity

Hides the pain of many leaves that have fallen from the trees

My poetry speaks loudly

And the words say nothing but temporary

Lessons that teach to deaf ears

As no one has time to listen

Too much turmoil to rescue me

I turned in my sanity and settled on insanity

As I continue to fight the battle that I lost long time ago

And I continue to fight

See in my mind the reality is that when I stop

The dirt begins to fall upon my grave

The headstone that reads silence

As no more will my words flow…..deep rivers

If I see one more headline
One more newscast
One more tear fall from a mother's eye
The kids that will never see mommy or daddy again
The scholarship that will never get used
The lawyer that almost was
Killing after killing
Abuse and more abuse
No one takes the blame
Too many reports still the same
And the numbers keep rising
I am passed the point that this is unacceptable
Politicians don't give a damn
Cops continue to take them down one at a time
And our children are gone way too soon
When will enough be enough?
Because last I checked it was enough when children
Like Emmett Till was killed
The church explodes and the four little girls died
Was that not enough
The slaves that their children were used as alligator bait
Is that enough…..enough was enough before we were born
I past that haunt us
When will it end?
Or do I lock my children inside

And strip them of the opportunities to live
As I am only protecting them so they don't die
Explaining to them when they ask why
Baby this is because we are not the same color
And they look at me bewildered
And hell to be honest so am I
I never have understood this
It makes no sense
They teach equality
And that amount to nothing but more lies
Lies that will forever follow
The home of the brave, land of the free
Forgot to include my reality
Unless you look at me with closed eyes
Your judgment starts and ends before I could begin
I am not a shade
I am not less than
I am not what you say I am
I am not owned by you
I am not beneath you
At the end of each day we are Kings and Queen
We are powerful and touched with Grace
I am who I am
The question is....Do you have a clue who you are?
My heart turned cold
Twisted fate

Forgiveness that only comes from one side
The darkness is darker than pass time
My strength driven into the ground
Raped of identity
Robbed of the last morsel of love
It no longer will be replenished
Solitude and the pain grows
Faster than lightning
I throw in the towel
Surrender the drippings that remain
The battle that was lost
The war conquered at the hands of yesterday
All that remains is silence

When the tears start

Someone screams stop

And the look on the inside boars

To the outside

What gives you the right the audacity?

To speak to me as if you know my story or even know me

Ink spills to the paper

From the inkwell of my past

My life

My ancestry

My history

Oh you wouldn't have a clue as to what that means

You are born from the backs of thieves

Day by day you continue to rid this earth of who I am

Because you don't like the likes of what stares at you

The history of hatred

Lies that begat lies

And rape laced with murder and you cry some form of defense

With little regard of life, the life of kings and queens

That walked this land

Own this land

My words flow between tears

As the wind blows and the cries are that of my ancestors

You have not a clue because your heritage is tainted

Pieced together off the backs of others

Never because of you…..deep rivers
One of my best friends is a police officer
She is an amazing woman of God
Will give her last
Fair is an understatement of her
Putting her life on the line to save others
And every day her life is in jeopardy
And my prayer has become
That she retires as soon as she can
My biggest fear
Is that her and other good cops like her
Die because of the bad ones
There is no excuse
No rhyme or reason why
Innocent children continue to die

Pain that runs so deep

Broken in many pieces

And that is the pain that crosses generation after generation

Down through the heritage of who we are

Or who we think we are

Not knowing the reality of what is supposed to be

The pain that plagues the heart

Dilapidated the soul

While suffocating the spirit of the once little child

That is all grown and still

The pain runs deep….

I truly am a mixture of sweet, honey, delectable dish...that waits....

but most of all yes I am that lemon meringue pie...

but you hit in the center of my heart with the perfect me...

Her core is solid black

Maybe others think not, but she has learned to ignore the simple minded

She knows her history of captured kin folk from the land of milk and honey

She is honey in red heart and yellow essence

She's hot to cool; her sway is black and brown spice

No, she is not almost something else

She is the one-drop rule that a person with any trace of African ancestry is... BLACK

To know me is to see pass the lemon deep

In the black core of my being....of...Who I Am....deep rivers

Oralipstic Talents

When my past.....
releases pieces of what....
will be.....
should decide.....
that deep desire.....
lust that battles with love.....
to taste the significance.....
while seducing what no longer sees.......
boundaries of flesh.....
pinned beneath....
flashes of light.....
as his tongue strips what control....
my mind thought it had.....
body betrayed.....
orgasms scream....
and flows fluently across his lips.....
as I fight to contained.....
but the pleasure....
demands more....
And all hell breaks loose......
as my past releases more pieces of my present....
only to await the future....
as his tongue drained my soul......deep rivers

My struggle is beyond the moon and passes the stars
Deep rooted issues that without answers the spiral will never end
The real truth is no answers will ever free me
No answers will solve the hurt that I feel
No possible answer to the question of why
Will ever solve the equation of my secret

Forgiveness for what
Forgiveness for whom
Forgiveness for why
Such that cannot be answered but constantly asked
And my past, continues to knock at my door

Your misty blue became my, "A change is going to come" in your hurt
With a splash of, "Walk on by"
I have walked in your shoes more than you even put your feet in them
And all I hear is forgive and move on
When will my melody start playing?
My African drum that beats a different beat

And the reality of all the bull
That has my heart on full, ready to explode
And walk away

Not missed by no means
Just the thought of new faces
That doesn't see my pain as I hide behind my mask of fame

I just want to walk away
Forward not backward
Still for moments to gain my breath
Never sideways
Pain

When will you ever go away?
Pain
And once again you appear
Pain
I need a break, maybe a vacation day
Pain
Only to realize that it will always be with me

But I have the choice of how it hurts or is it only the glue to my past
As I truly believe that if I don't know where I come from
How will I know where I'm going?
Yet another phrase that comes and goes
Sounds good
But hurts so bad
Living in a world that doesn't provide blinders….deep rivers

My body went into overload
My mind went into shutdown mode
And my spirit wanted to slap the next one that walked in her path
And that was just today's thoughts
No understanding of what just took place
As you seem to think I am irrelevant
Questioned from start to finish
What should be?
What is to be?
And what the hell wasn't
You moaned and groaned and called my name many times
And then you had the audacity to say don't get attached
Last time I checked I never called out your name
And if I did I know how to handle
I know what may turn into a scandal
And if it does
Believe me I can take care of all that I dish back
Forward and slow grind at you
You said what you didn't want
What you had no desire to have
And all I could say was who are you trying to convince
And believe me it was not me because
I was there
From the moment you tasted more than my emotions
And I returned the favor

And tasted all of yours

As you called out my name

And it was meant to be just that way

Because I like you

Enjoyed more than just your conversation

I enjoyed you

And you didn't have a clue

What was before you and let walk on by

I scream yet again

I made a mistake again

You become part of my sin

But why can I not get you out of my mind

My head

My thoughts

Your taste on my lips

That sets me on fire every time I lick them

The strokes

The way you looked at me

The compliments you gave

You made me feel like a desired woman all over again

And yes it has been awhile

And you want me to forget

All of that?

Why in the hell did you ever taste my emotions in the first place…..deep rivers

So many ask how….why….did you stay

I look back and I only see my silence

The voice of reason was suffocating, not allowed to speak

Have you ever walked into a door that wasn't there?

Back to the beginning…..

The moment our eyes met

The words that screamed at me

I knew that I would finally be free

I didn't see what was being planned right before me

My death

I was treated like a Queen

Showered with gifts, love and affection

So how did the tables turn?

My light slowly drifted away

The darkness walked in and commanded to be recognized

He had turned all that I knew into

All that I swore never to be a part of

See I was raised in a house where constant beating was common

Not common for you but definitely common for me

I saw it happen over and over and then it happened to me

The constant abuse that I became to know as routine

So when I dated I swore never to allow it to swing my way

And it never did

Until we were married and then

I walked into walls, doors and a table here and there

Yes that was always the reason why

I had the black and blue eyes

And they ask why did I stay?

He whispered in my ear softly …..I will kill you

He whispered in my ear softly …..I love you

He whispered in my ear softly …..It's your fault that I hit you

And then he screamed what happen, who did this!!

Yes he acted as if he had no clue

Ranting about what he would do if he found the person who did this

I wanted to scream, It was you!!!

But my fear and isolation had rendered me silenced

My voice no longer spoke

I started to believe his lies

Covering the black eyes

It lasted until he snapped at my child

And that I could not take

I stepped outside of me and….

Broke my silence and refused to be

I screamed hit me but never my child

And then I knew it was time to go

My child will never have to show

The signs of my abuse passed down

So I gave my voice sound

No longer to be silenced again…..

So many are afraid to speak….the process of isolation and losing their self-esteem makes them think they are at fault and doomed to live this….Domestic Violence will always Need A Voice…to no longer be Silenced…deep rivers

Bludgeoned Quest

Once again I look in the mirror
And the tears blur the vision of what should be
I only see the hurt that once again
Again I say
Has fallen upon my shoulders
I no longer look to the light
The darkness that consumes me
Suffocating on the air in your own lungs
Not that of another
That which you are exposed to
My dark side
Not many understand and won't ever understand
The pain for pleasure
The pleasure for pain
That seems to find me
I don't go in search for what even I can't truly explain
Collaborating with my sin
That continues to stand face to face with my demons
Demons that are mine because of the darkness that consumes
Me…
Given to me by those that strangle the air I breathe
The pain inflicted by others
Scarred for life

And the knife that just seems to be passed from hand to hand
Then reinserted into the same pain
Never healed
Never gone
Never whole again
My reality
My nightmares are as common as most dreams
And the repeat button
Goes on and on
And on
As I drop to my knees
Wondering why
Asking the same damn questions over and over
When will my light shine
And to be honest, I never receive an answer
The clouds take control and darkness prevails
A soul that has been beaten and abused
To the point that pain is my reality……deep rivers

"Chameleon's Interlude"

Nobody has a clue or do they
The rush that fuels my flames
Intensifies my fire and craving that I must have
He is my addiction
As I am his
Submissive in every since of the word
And his eyes let me know that I am his drug
Submissive yes, but I hold the power in the palm of my hand
His energy drained as my needs are strong
I feel each stroke and I want more
With each lick, I need his tongue to rendezvous with all of me
Tasting every flavor that rests upon my flesh
As his flesh, wet and hot, drenched with the sweat of me
Pheromones that reached the top of the hill and cascade down the other side
And yes I am his submissive, but he is my toy
Then darkness arrives and the flesh
All alone needing to be caressed
And your voice appears before you
And I close my eyes and venture into another hidden surprise
The darkness that brought pure chocolate to my door
Yes he arrived and my fear stayed on the other side of that closed
Door....

Yes stripped and devoured with no words spoken

Sweet chocolate with a swirl of honey to accompany it

He licked and I sucked and wrapped myself in pure darkness

That I didn't want light to shine upon

Yes he fed me all the flavors that his body could sustain

And then the explosion happened

He dripped cream all over my honey and the flavor we created

Our own sweet Honey Do….

My appetite needed to be satisfied and yet I still

Need

Want

And desire

The flavor that only exists in my dreams

If only I could sleep in my fantasy until it becomes my

Reality

My here and now

The end to my beginning

The dam to the river that flows

But only in my dreams…….deep rivers

Emotional Massage

I needed him to caress away my pain
Kiss the fears that arise deep from within
To taste pass my flavor
He tasted my emotions
Fell to my knees in tears
While I waited for love to see my desires
As they appeared in my eyes
Lost from my heart
But nestled in the heat of my thighs
Fear of loneliness
Fear of failure
Fear of abandonment
But most of all
The fear that no one sees
Fear of self.....deep rivers

Kiss me until my pain smiles back....deep rivers

Love's Footnote

I want you to love me now

Love me tomorrow

Love me when I forget to love myself

But most of all, allow me to love you......deep rivers

If it ain't one thing it's another….
That tune plays over and over in my head
And damn no matter what I can't get it to stop
Mind on overload
Caught in the catch 22 of life
Not knowing if I am coming or going
Hell lost
Directions evade me at this point
East west north or south
And all I can do is stand still
Do I go left when my feet go right?
Or do I walk in circles?
Struggling use to be a problem shared by many but damn
Here lately the struggle has turn to drowning on a sip of water
Suffocating on air that no longer even exists
Hell I realize ain't nothing free. Even the air we breathe
So I sit here with my head in my hands
Contemplating my next move and I draw a blank
Nothing
Absolutely nothing
And then I hear a voice
One that is so familiar
That the tears stream down my face
Baby, listen please
The room became silent and she continued

Baby we got this!!

Ain't never left your side

Been right by your side

We have traveled up down hell all around for that matter

But we did it together never alone

So as far as I'm concerned nothing has changed

We got this….

I got you as much as you have me

See this ain't never been 50/50

It's always 100% on both sides of the fence

And when one falls short the other always comes through

You got me and baby yes, I got you……

Am I feeling all that is present

Does he feel me

Thoughts of him

Reliving the first words that touched

Reaching so far down in the pit of my soul

the essence of all things right or wrong

not knowing which but non the less wanting

to fly free as sky above

to taste

the sweetness of sweet mangoes

juice flowing

flowing quenching more than a thirst

but a need that has never ended

and needed to be fed

touch me

with a soft caress like the petals of an African violet

as my heart beats stronger than a African drum

I crave

what I have yet to find

or have I

so far

but so close

and still I crave....deep rivers

Through the Looking Glass

The reality has not changed

Color of my skin

is still the sin of the day

my sin

and all that are darker than butter

or black as coal

the issue is

Black is beautiful

and the darker the berry the sweeter

more than just juice

Educated

never duplicated

Energetic

and I am

tired of being apologetic

but

no more

Why should I not love all that I am

Proud of who I am

The way I look

my ancestry

history

of more than what

they choose to tell

teach

and the teacher needs the failing

grade

for not telling the truth

Slavery is Not

who we are

it is what we endured

Kings and Queens

and that hasn't changed

Stare in the mirror

and you will see all that you are you

were just conditioned not to believe

Stop believing in a system

that was never meant for you and me

and research you reality

We accept what others teach us

instead of teaching ourselves

Six in one hand, half a dozen in the other

Stop believing everything you see on TV

Believe in your written

proven

on the back of many

history

be proud of who you are

everything else is a wanna be
never the true me....A Beautiful Black Queen

Destiny's Soul Search

He whispered.....I found my soul mate
and my thoughts were the same
I couldn't respond as my smile was in full bloom
The moment when all seems so right
or is it wrong
but feels right
I haven't determined that
I just know that at that moment
that second
in time
I felt like a butterfly
flying free
and high
above all
that once mattered
Realizing that life
is truly to be lived
enjoyed
discovering the intricate secrets
of someone
the one
who

made

you feel

more than alive

real

without the games

the deception

delusion

His words were real

concrete

the black rose

the bloomed in hard reality

he saw pass

all that and made me smile....deep rivers

Misunderstanding of My Understanding

His words….

Brought tears streaming through my soul

A lump of coal in my throat

And heartache that couldn't be explain

Nothing prepared me for this

Nothing ever does

Jolted with lightning

Slapped with life's realities

Or what they call reality

I want to have a cute put it in a box and wrap it excuse

But

No amount of words

Seem

To fit

The tears

Or the fact that they are flowing so fast

And I am not quite sure why

But they still

Flow down my face

Flow from my soul

Leaving desertion in the pit

Of my spirit

I still

Need to know

Why

When

And by chance did I miss the memo

On hurt

Yet again

His words stuck on repeat

Repeat

Repeat

And I still can't bring myself to hit the stop button

They play over

And

Over

And still the jolt of lightning

Still electrifies my thoughts

Yeah caught on repeat

I feel his

Pain

Which causes my tears….to continue….deep rivers

"Phantom's Hope"

My tears....

The constant stream of.....

Tightening of my heart.....

Eyes closed....

Lost in the sensuality. ....

Of his words.....

Strength that gave light to my....

Darkness.....

A smile appeared....

And then....

Something. ....

Changed.....

While my heart stays the same....

Hear the whispers of.....

What is to be true....

Or am I just confused.....

Reading what is not there....

Blank pages....

Of emotions.....

Again.....deep rivers

The Rebirth of Love's Orientation

I want to taste you beneath the rainbow of reality
Lick your tears before they decide to fall
My reality has turned into more than a lifetime movie
As of this
Very
Moment
The reality
I have fallen
For the reality of your dreams
Kiss me
So that
I
Know its
Real
You reached far inside
Of the spectrum that
Creates the dreams that I keep sealed
And you
Opened a cocoon that will soon be
Beautiful butterflies
Flying over the emotions
Of my soul
Give and you shall receive

Deceive

And

The tears will fall from your very own

Eyes

My love is that of a dreamer

Wanted more than most will

Ever

Ever

Receive

Strokes that come down strong and hard

But bring the softness of a beautiful flower

With the pouring rains

Of my

Orgasms

And

I request more

And

More

Fluttering

To the head

Of your

Imagery

Taste me

Absorb

My spirit

With yours

As we

Become one

Entity

Facing the world of destiny....deep rivers

"In the Folds of the Creators Hands"

Heart strings pulled

Tugged and damn near strangled

Emotions the size of the world and they are tossed in the rivers

Of misunderstanding

Clues that tell a tall tale

False representation

Strung along

With the possibility of nothing

Love has never played fair

Throwing delusional

Imagery across the hearts of many

And you ask why

The struggle to love again

Even when the hurt is more than one can bare

Raped of one's identity

Retreating to what hides the broken smiles

The bruised lips

Believing in the whispers of love

Knowing that the chance to be unconditionally happy

Only

Exists

In

Fairytales

And last I checked
Age expired on that a long time ago
But you have hope
And prayer that this time
Around
Maybe
Only it never
Happens
But maybe
This will be different
God's call
The purpose for your soul
Loved in many ways
Shackled by the needs and wants
Of a simple smile
To laugh from way down deep
Reality is
That once again a heart that has been used
And thrown back
His words released all the pain
And his hands rescued you from what was
To restore faith and hope again….deep rivers

"Willing Prisoner…..Unwilling Victim"

I opened up

Allowed him to slip in

Under my deepest dreams

Not just the surface

He went deep

His words rest upon my breast

As each letter slowly trickled down the length of me

Finding their way to my hidden treasure

I allowed him in

So I can't

Won't

Be

Even though

I want to

Be

Mad at him

See the reality is that his lips

Never touched mine

They took them captive

With each melody that he placed in my heart

Hopes and dreams

That

He laid out for the two of us

And in all actuality

He hit the switch so quick

That I never saw it coming

And refuse to believe

What my ears felt

I really don't know what to say

Or do

I just know

At this very

Moment

He holds my heart hostage

With no release in sight

When poetry deceived me

I lost the battle

So who will win the war?.....deep rivers

Soul's Canvas and Clay

I need to paint

Splashes of color wherever they may land

Brush in hand

My pain

Needs

To

Take

Shape

My life a blur of color

Tossed about with little hope

Of direction

Abstract

No rhyme or reason

Just release of color

As my eyes see nothing but tears

From pain

Hurt

Trials and tribulations

That slowly

Sculpt

This piece of art

A masterpiece

Deep from the soul

Of constant hurt

Deception

Delusion

Words that float from one

And land on my ears

And burn my lips

Fire

Heat of passion

I close my eyes

Only to open them to see

What colors?

Describe me

And the emotions that take flight

Through my masterpiece…..deep rivers

"Twin Mystiques Curtain Call"

I dropped my head years ago
Never to return
I put her to rest
Out of her misery
Yes she put up a hell of a fight but she loss
The battle to me
Insecurity
No self esteem
She just couldn't figure out how to love her
We went round after round
And she wouldn't go down
So I whispered in her ear these words
I have enough love for the both of us
You brought us this far
Now pass the torch
I am you and you are me
But what is most important
Listen clear
I have enough love for the both of us
When the doctors diagnosed this or that
You cried
I fought even her
When you were ridiculed

You cried

And my tongue became that much swifter

At the moment of your despair

I held you hand

Even dragged you if I had to

Because I meant my words

I have enough love for the both of us

You are me and I am you

And with the two of us

You can rest

The battle has been won

And now I know that I have won the war

When I look deep in the mirror

I see the true beauty that you nurtured

That is the beauty that I provide a backbone for

Your tears will continue to stream

Because God gave you a heart of gold

But tears only when necessary

Please let her rest

As I am in control now

And I know you are always just a whisper away

We know every trial and tribulation we go through

Only makes us stronger

You are me and I am you

And yes I got enough love for the both of us…..deep rivers

"Unbalanced Prowess"

Deception lives at darkness door
Delusion or is it illusion
Winter storm in the middle of summer time
And yet you still want to believe
That which stares back
Is stronger than before
Lilies in the valley
Never to reach full bloom
As the water to quench their thirst
Ceases to come
And the sunlight
Hidden behind darkness door
Suffocating on an inch of water
You thought would nourish the fields
Once again
What was
Is not
And what
Should be
Has been laughed off stage
Words that tell the tale
Yet again
And you

Still

Believe

A half empty glass or half full

Either way will you drink what

Is left

To quench your thirst

Or will you wade in what is not there

What is real

Has become my favorite game

Chess

And yes

Without the power of the queen

You may end up in checkmate

Or that which you doubted

The pawns at hand

May win it all…..deep rivers

I sat in the corner of my mind

slowly I dissected

dismantled

a heart

of emotions

I climbed

the ladder

of understanding and

all that remained

was broken pieces of who she was

lost in the pain of who she has become

not knowing the outcome

of each day

some days

better

than others

and the reality is

pain has become the corner of my minds

instruction

love to love

as his soft words

heal an abandoned light

walking on the dark side

of

my eyes

seeing

the valley over

the trees

I am my worst enemy

and you are my best deed

love me over the moon

as you kiss me where my thighs

meet

in the realm of knowing

what is

Penned....Deep Rivers

The mind that never rest

the

music

plays

a different tune

than the sounds around me

trapped in the moment

of

reality

fighting to reach

fantasy

but

he

is

so damn

far away to touch

but I feel all that he is

I feel him more than he feels his self

Talented with gifts that

shine

but can he walk on

the dark

side

of

where

I reside

sweat dripping

heat rising

with a tongue bath that misses not one

special

spot

hot from the stirring of what he fears

to dive deep

in rivers

that flow

giving life

beyond any that he has ever known

he whispers

and it is done

pleasure placed

from the top to the tip of his soul

yes words

started a fire

that will forever burn

the fantasy

that

has

now

become the reality that leaves him speechless

Deep rivers a continuous flow of ecstasy....

Pursuit of Exclusivity

Slip into the den of misunderstanding

words that don't need

to be

explained

as you

know

exactly

the true

meaning of deception

delusion

within my own eyes

desire

that lives behind

the cornea

waiting

contemplating

the next

move

that needs to be made

heights to reach

in the clouds of

the impossible

and I still reach for all that is there

my instincts keen

and never blind

to what is before me

know and trust

the mind of a word master

reading between

behind

and over the words that spill so gracefully

to the pages

your cockiness

will have you miss the reward

that most never receive

tired

drained

as my mind never seems to rest

as greatness is just over the valley

and my eyes will not rest until it is mine

slip into the den of understanding.....deep rivers

Conscious Fluidity

Inspiration that flows deep

into the valley

and then all over us

flowing like melted chocolate

ready to lick every drop

the reality is

hot

amazing

graphics

that create imagery

that makes juices stir

and nectar flow

waiting as he catches every drop

of who I am

words that speak volumes

with a mere whisper

eyes that speak to your soul

words that write the smooth ending to tragedy

and in the same breath

breathe life into what once was gone

inspiration that strips your of any hidden fears

power play

he is that and so much more....inspiration

The Love Letter....response By Deep Rivers

You sent me a letter that quite frankly swelled the tears in my eyes and the lump in my throat

see for me love has always came hard

I love hard and always pay the price with my emotions splattered again

So as I read you words

I ponder can it be, is it possible for one to really love

Me

to feel the love

that I give from deep within

never to walk away,

my love will die for his

I give until the well runs dry

so I ask myself does he feel my love

To share a friendship

that battles between our beliefs

as we will agree to disagree

to understand that

I love you means

I am not alone and neither are you

To feel my heat rise

my words whispered

that land on your lips

swallowed in the pit of your soul

simple but complex words

meaning the protection of my heart

See

I slowly watched my eyes fall in love

with you

my heart get encased in your hands

as my hope to love again

for infinity

not the moment

I knew when I said the words out loud

You would hear me whisper

I Love You.

Or did you hear at all situations

That complicate what can be only if we let them

I see you in my dreams that bring me heat

Causing my breathing to go astray

Wanting you to take me

I almost believed what was not real

I knew then that my broken heart needed

To be healed so that the love that came for

A lifetime stay

can stay with

She wants more than the physical One

A quest to obtain the physical with

The spiritual love which goes deep

For the two

She believes as her soul comes back

To life with the kiss of his spirit they are love...

"Elusive Love Shadows"

As the eyes of delusion

Walk through my soul

False representation

Of a love gone wrong

Never being honest with your own heart

While playing an unknown melody

With the emotions that bloom

From the valley of intuition

Kiss of darkness

Dimming the light of hope

While waiting

For the sun to return

You ask

Or assume

And neither gives

Reality responses

As you are faced with a heart

Laced in gold

Lips that give life

With arms that rock away

All the pain of yesterday

A gift so great

Precious

And open to explore
The battle of which way to go
As heart strings
Pull in many ways
Waiting on the right way
To be.....love given while waiting on return
Love to love....deep rivers

"Erogeneous Winds of Euphoria"

The storm is full blown
The music plays a melody
That only are souls take in
Feel
Breathe in
Bodies stir with intensity
To clear the dance floor
As those that watch
Take notes
Your eyes
Dictate all that my body does
Your touch heats
More than my soul
It gives life to mine
Bringing my soul alive
You escape into my deepest dreams
Walking through my fantasies
And complete the orgasms
To explosion
Watering the flowers that bloom
In the darkest of night
But with a kiss of light
As the valley flourishes

With your words

The light in your eyes

Know that nothing else

Can be

What I deliver

The aroma that entices the room

Dressed in the colors

That bring passion

To what we have

The darkness to light

Is what we are.....deep rivers

"The Perseverance of Fantasy's Truth"

The depth of your desires

The will to make it be all that it can

To push forward

When negative rears it's head

And you continue to grow

Reaching for

Not accepting less

Giving from one's soul

As I listen to the whispers

That speak

Guidance

Direction

And complete need

Of satisfaction

The flower that blooms

From cement

With ever changing color

A smile that shines

Through the darkness

Who am I?

"Footsteps of Maturity "

So many walk by the wrong rules of life
No we are not perfect
Mistakes made by us all
and if someone says they haven't made any
Walk away in silence
Why debate what you know is a lie
Someone said that Karma came to visit
Stayed and decided to be a permanent resident
for them not me
I packed and moved on
I will not allow something or someone that does not pay any bills
to take up residence in my head
Today's mistakes
Are the lesson's
For tomorrow's adventure
I will not be complacent
or blame self for a mistake that is gone
Not to return
That would be the same as debating with the one who says
they never made a mistake
Only a fool argues with themselves
Karma walks on the other side of the street....deep rivers

"Web of Regrets"

My emotions float on the unbiased seas

Giving a false sense of what many

Have not a clue

As they indulge in the surface of their reality

None that concerns the hurt that even they create

Words spewed into the atmosphere that cannot be

Retracted

There aren't any such things as take backs

See you never slowed the engine

Long enough to see the sword that you wielded

Into the heart of

Back of

In the eyes that you know longer stare into

Situations that only complicate

You hit erase

Disowned

The one who you chose to treat as a complete stranger

Lies that you told

Not to me but on you

Fairy tales do come true

When you trust Kings not devils that masquerade around

Dressed in the cloak of deception

Your words are that of the lies that you have convinced yourself

As the sky surely comes in shades of blue
Your lies offer the comfort that only come in deep shades of red
Splattered back and forth across the horizon of yesterday
And you continue
Such a sad case that does not know for if and only if
You would still continue to lie
As it is deep inside of you
The wiring that only you can change
You are your own electrician to your soul
Will you re-wire or electrocute yourself and those that stand too close
The disdain for one who lies
I would rather walk in the truth than
Wade in a lake of lies
So many see the quick fix of lies as the quick fix to a broken soul
All that it provides is permanent hurt, for the one that continues to lies….deep rivers

The Dream of My Soul....Dawn.....

Deep there is a dream in my soul
One that gives many things
A repetitive dream that floats above reality
See my dream has always been to answer
The question Who am I ?
Does that make sense?
To ask the question at my age?
Well along the way, not to far back
I went in search of answers
I realized the question was more complexes
Than I could ever even imagine....
See what seems to be simple with
The answer that brings about a bountiful of
More questions
My question challenged my worth value,
Substance that I thought I knew
So many don't understand pass
The surface of what our D.N.A IS
See what I thought for many years
Was thrown into the sea of misery
My eyes stared back at me and
For some other reason....
I saw a blank canvas and

The masterpiece that it should be
Didn't appear
What is rightfully mind or so
I thought was lost in the secrecy of others
No one knew that I walked in a shadow
My own shadow
The steps that I take directed
My the dream of my soul
The D.N.A opened the book
To even more questions of
Who am I?
As I walk through the dream of my soul

"The Eulogy of Embattled Love

I picked up my pen and the only word....
that made it to the paper was silence....
laid my hands on the keyboard....
and the only word I could type was silence...
my heart....mind...spirit and soul...went silent.....
as I slowly gathered my thoughts.....
he said things that stung....
no I have to be honest....
they hurt....
and then I realized that the hurt wasn't mine....
it was and is his....
his pain greater than the naked eye....
see the words that he said....
I had to direct them back at him...
the distaste that he thought he had for me....
was for him....
as I know exactly what I taste like...
and the smile is upon my face....
one he will never know....
I am my words....
an addict of many things....
and sex is at the top of the list....
fighting a battle with words.....

I make no excuses for who I am....

as I listened to his....

and deep down the tears flowed....

I cleansed my soul yet again....

and walked away.....

My weakness is stronger than your strength.....deep rivers

"Emotional Clairvoyance"

The depth of my inner mind....

runs away at times with thoughts...

that give me many words....

many emotions...

the ability to see....

what is not there....

to taste the flavor....

that I go in search.....

that searches for me.....

to experience love and warmth.....

that caresses....

strokes the curve of my face.....

holds the imperfections that are perfect at the right time....

I am the epitome of love...

the desire of want.....

and the capability of need....

see as the moon glows over the sun in my eyes....

that bleeds understanding....

a heart of now....deep rivers

"The Armored Core of Love "

Roots the start of a strong foundation
Placed first
As he prepares himself to be the protector
The guidance
Inner piece
As his thoughts of logic
Venture to the beauty that he seeks
His Queen
She gives him life beyond his own
As he cradles her soft, caressed face
To give certainty that he is and will be
Her King
The strength that she can depend on
The healer of her tears
While they build one brick at a time
Knowing that she strokes him at times of exhaustion
She is his backbone of life
He is she and she is him
Hand in hand the cross the lines of capabilities
As they strive together
Never alone
They are

She is his life while he is her strength
Feeding him the nectar of her labor
As he quenches his thirst with her intuition
They are and will be
One plus one equals one
Together hand in hand....

Deep Rivers

Title and review

Awesome warrior, tired, but willing, strong chin, ailing backbone, dented shield, chipped blade, grit, heart, despite setbacks, always ready to do battle........

"The Bravado of My Weary Shadows"

My soul is tired
Spirit strong but is it strong enough to fight
To feel or not to feel
The moments that flash before my eyes
Chances to get it right
And all that I knew was I wanted to survive
See, what looks one way may not be
What the naked eyes see or even believes
My soul is tired
And my spirit refuses to give up
Even when all of my tears have dried up and gone away
See what the naked eye sees
Is nowhere near the pain that rears from behind the shadow
Eloquence is not for the hands that don't move
Precision is not for the pain that never misses a beat
My heart cries to the heavens
Waiting for the pain to subside and the normal to begin again
As I know no other way

I know not how but that I have to
See what many never see
Is the disease that slowly takes its toll
I fight back
And at times I win
Or I win in my mind
But doesn't ever go away
I smile with each day
That I see the sun rise
And set over the horizon of understanding
As the moon dims the light so that I can see
The sun heats my face but stings the skin I am in
No one knows
Because the smile is the smile they see
They don't realize that it is upside down
For the frown is truly me
As the pain takes its toll
On me
I don't know no other way but to be
Continuously moving forward
As backwards never works for two left feet
I cry with the smile of my tears
And the strength of knowing that to stop
Means that I give up
And giving up ain't never been a part of me
I go on

As if the naked eye can't see

The pain that consumes me

I don't know no other way to be….deep rivers

"Anticipation of Waiting"

His hands were the brushstrokes of my soul.....
delicate strokes that tiptoe through my tulips......,
while my soul stirred with the capability of what is....
he doesn't know....
doesn't feel the rush....
of the sunlight that reaches out across the sea of contemplation....
in the meantime a heart waits for adoration.....
cultivation of mental thoughts....
that supersedes all understanding....
he is...
will be....
while wet kisses......
that have yet to be received....
bring a smile to a heart that is waiting.....deep rivers

Once upon a time

Only in my mind

There is no once upon a time in my head

All that exists

Is wants

Needs

And tears

That never ceases to appear

Without the reality of what is

And then a pen

Crossed

My many thoughts

Punctuating my dreams

And hyphenating

My reality

The ink bled in many colors

Of hope

Peace

And love from the depths of an ink well

That never runs dry

The possibilities are infinite

The battle that

Will right

Or write

Its own ending

Or maybe not

But the path shall not

Go without the caresses of my pen

The seduction

Of whom I am

And all that hibernates

Deep

Will rise and dance with…..sensational lines…..deep rivers

A childhood that continues to live on
In my dreams and reality
see no matter what I do now
the nightmares of what was
play over and over
in my mind
the childhood that was stripped
taken
ripped
from the
heart of a
child
never to be given back
you crept in the night
but your damage lives in daylight
chained to the disgrace of you
your demented mind that took
from me
and now I have to be
chained to the disgrace of you
for life
but the one piece of the puzzle
that you didn't have
was I stayed chained

to those memories

to protect my offspring

from never walking in the darkness

of demented minds like you

I will never allow

them to be stripped

of a childhood

as I was

chained as a remembrance

of minds like you

powerful that it will never

happen again.....

deep rivers

The reality of a facade is more than a storm at midnight

Seeing the trees for the forest

And getting wet all the same

Can you feel the connection of two souls?

Pulling in the same direction

Wanting to taste the flavor

Of emotions that spill to the pages

As the suns attempts to shine through raindrops

But the wind spins them into destiny

He feels hers lips play a melody up and down

The length of his steel

While his hands caress the melons that accentuates her curves

She feels the vibrations with each touch

The heat from his hands is more than the sun

Upon her face

All a while the raindrops fall

Never cooling off the heat that has taken over her

Slowly they both undress

Each other

And lips continue on a journey of what pleasures them the most

He listens has her breathing increases

As his hand finds her nectar

That spills for him

He clutches her

She wraps her fingers around him

And they both stroke each other to the rhythm of the raindrops

As the sun peeks through to be the spotlight

Of their show

Better than Broadway

As they continue

Building each other to the explosion of a lifetime

The moans escape

From the two of them

As the moment has arrived

They both release

With screams of ecstasy

He is her

And she is him

At the moment they both give

And receive at the same time

Raindrops the back drops to the pleasure

That has started and they will continue

The moment in time

That created a connection between two souls

Never to be duplicated

As they are now one……deep rivers

If I wrote a love letter....

where would I start...

would it be complex....

or would it be simple....

I decided the complex simple way....

I love you....

deep rivers

"Solitaire's Paradox"

Have you ever wondered?

Sat back and surveyed the situation

Rewind

From the beginning to the end

How you can be in a room full of friends

And still be lonely

Look at the many calls

The multiple texts

And still be lonely

The warm yet cold body

That lies next to you and yet

You still feel lonely

Nothing seems just right

Or the puzzle always ends up with a missing piece

The many moments of why

When

Where

Did I go wrong?

What

Is wrong with me

Or is anything at all

See so many never face reality, the cold truth

The eyes that stare back as you ask these questions

Because to be honest who really wants to hear the answers
Face the cold reality
The one plus one
That for you always equals just two
Not the answer of one, when two souls are joined
Or the common misunderstanding
That what you thought it was
Wanted it to be was nothing more
Than what they needed
Damn what you needed
Or thought you could give or receive
See we go back to the beginning
How do you stand in a room full of friends and still
Feel lonely……deep rivers

Moments when I wanted to give up

To walk away and just accept

The single life that was before me

And then

He walked into my life

I had no clue

That which was before me may be

For me

Conversations that left me wanting for the next call

Words that reached

Twisted

And soothed all at the same time

I couldn't explain

But I felt myself drawn to the mystery

Not knowing if I should approach

Or keep my fantasy in my head

And accept the reality that he wasn't available

He had no clue

None whatsoever that the voice at the other end of the line

Was wishing upon a star

Hoping for

Looking towards

That which I never thought

Would

Could

Come true

We talk and the flutters of butterflies

Dance

The smile never leaves

As the warmth continues to reach degrees

That only he has been capable of doing

He had not a clue

And I still don't know if he really knows

How much I enjoy

The smiles he gives

To look into his eyes

Being wrapped in his arms

As our hearts beat in sync

He is…..

"In Time, Our Space, and My Visibility "

I sit in the darkness

Examining the visions that haunt

My reality

Illusions creep in through the slice of sunshine

Only to see it disappear before my very own eyes

The dream that I was not destined to have

While reaching for the next one

The words that forever sit at the base of my

Intuition of life

Answering the invisible questions

With time

That transcends understanding into a cloud of the here and now

See it takes the abilities that are from the realm of control

Light faster than sound

Or is the sound of my voice faster than the light you extinguished

inside of me

I am was will shall be the blossoming future of our lives

Deep Rivers

External Gratification

She slipped under him and allowed him to pin her to his will
She is submissive
Destined for happiness
As well as the happiness received from pleasing him
Walked into today with satisfaction from yesterday
With the want to capture the future dreams with him
More than the sexual gratification that he gives
Ability to read the books that have yet to be written
She is the epitome of seduction
As he waits for the moment, when she falls to her knees
To please him, swallowing all that he is
She needs to be needed
While he needs her to please, Erotically
His words cultivate inside her
Direct the path to find
Sensual, passionate and pleasure to not only her body
But starting with her mind
The heat that never goes out
Fire that intensifies her desires for wanting to be loved
Loneliness sits guardian over the entrance to past tomorrow
She stands still in silence
Waiting

The intricate parts of understanding

Knowing the ins and outs of confusion

With the pleasure of why

I cannot see pass the trees

Or into the darkness with eyes wide shut

My heart has closed with no chance of

Whatever happens next

Will the time just pass by

No need for an answer to a problem

Or a question with reasons

It is not for the faint at heart

But it is my reality

And

That

Is

All I have…..deep rivers

Voluptuous thoughts that are mere ideas

Thick in all the right places

With a desire to drip sugar and spice

That takes you on a sugar high

Blacked out to

What should have been?

And knowing that the steps were

On the path to hell

Not the path that I should have stepped on

The golden road that has been laced with hot coals

Plastered with lies and misfortunes

Battery of what one stands for

And the answers never answer the questions at hand

See what really is what

Why

How or just that

Jumbled words that depending on the eyes

That gazes upon them

May decide if they have meaning

Or just what they are

Many letters that fall to the ground

Never landing

As they continue to stir

And create more

Misfit questions

In search of

With the threat

Of never finding…..deep rivers

His scent caused my daydreams

While lips captured my nights

He is more than I tried not to calculate

Into an equation of misunderstandings

I carefully continued to give all the reasons why

I don't even remember the question

See he found a light

Hidden behind tears of constant failure

And still he repeated over and over again

The beauty that he saw, beauty within

A soul that holds the pages of a lifetime

Written then tossed and written again

And the ink has not even bled onto the pages

Nor has this book been completed

As he refuses to put her in a box

He knows that she must continue to fly free

Not the ordinary

Extraordinary is all he sees

And he knows that her freedom

Allows for her creative to flourish

Continue

Without hesitation

And she

Always

Flies

Home

To the one who saw what no one else did…..deep rivers

He slipped deep into darkness

That caused the stirring of what

Slept in the dark

The physical battled with the mental

Over what was the spiritual?

That supersedes reality

His direction with strokes

Of pain and pleasure

That continued even when

He walked out with a

Possibility of no return

I slipped and fell once again

Spiraling out of control and the hope of

Landing fell with me

I fell in love and didn't know when love decided

To visit my heart

As for now I walk

With feet that never touch the ground

How many times

Words hurled at you

Laughter at you not with you

Degradation

Abuse

Ridicule

Badgered

Put Down

Criticized

over and over

over and over

again

to the point that your soul is tired

but the blessing is

that you

see you

when no one

else

sees

but the beauty continues to exist

Always see the true you

through it all....deep rivers

Contemplating the reasons why

The moments of how

And the opportunity of where

Will the chance

Become circumstance

Or the dance

Of direction

The spill of words

With meaning or

Simply just words

Purposely directed when the curtain call

Rises

Or falls

Life is more than trials and tribulations

It is the ingredients that you choose

The sugar and spice

With a dash of heat

To balance and awaken the rhythm inside

For without my words

I shall drown on a sip of water

While suffocating on pure existence

Words that carry the weight of the world

Or a voice

That hears in silence

The battle to never let my ink dry out

Deep Rivers

Love of a Woman

She is love

Wet kisses of emotion

The grip of her thighs

Add to the strength of her building foundation

Juices that flow with each orgasm

The glue of substance that holds down who she is

And what she builds

With

You

And in you

She is the infinite book of continuous learning

Given the opportunities to build create and construct greatness

Her touch soft as an African violet

With tenacity to forever evolve

She taste you with the desire of the heart

No temporary pleasure

Pleasure that builds fires

Creating a bond of survival of what is now hers

She stands tall

With you as the erection of faith

Nothing is impossible

With a woman that is given and receives unconditional love

She is

The wet kisses of emotion

Educated with the ability to continue to learn

She possesses passion sensuality and strength

With velvet touch strokes

That gives

Never to be under estimated

For she will walk away

But to love her

Is a gift that she receives and continues to give back freely

The love of a woman

That loves unconditionally

The hidden secret in an open book
Sequestered in mind travel
Juices flow within a barrier of sound
Screams of passion that fall in the valley
While contemplation battles the moment
Checkmate of a wounded soul
Hidden in plain sight
Stolen jewels of understanding
Never mind the same time in the darkness
For the light dances to the moon

Deep Rivers

"Forgotten Shadow's Breakthrough"

As the darkness no longer a factor

I surfaced to the realization of today

See at many points on the daily ritual

I see the possibilities that may

Come and go

But whatever comes to stay

The joy that has been slammed into a closet

That fights to be released

But the chains of loneliness

Is more than physical

The mental bondage

Catapults ones soul

Deeper into what seems impossible to escape

My mind with closed eyes

See the future and what it holds

But the struggle to reach

What is not within ones reach?

But it is

Steps to accurately review the path

Before me

No one has a clue

The tortured soul

Never rests

I know that which lies in the universe of

Understanding

Or is it misunderstanding

As the catalyst that should be

No longer have I armed reach

See the continuous growth

Seems to cause the pain that

My heart feels

That my eyes see

Crumbs that laced my lips

That feed nothing's

The hunger real

The deprivation that floats in my identity

No one sees the pain that

Never rests

As the truths never seem to be

Walking backwards in a sideways world

Trapped in a closet with no doors

While standing still

As my travels encompass the universe

Love has never been erected on rotten timber

In the midst of the storm

The rain continues to fall

While the earth provides new trees

To see through

Deep Rivers

My thoughts faster than light

with the tears of evolution

See I know that growth brings about change

But for me the pains that creep deep pour like

A spring thunderstorm

I am in my thoughts

my mind filled with tug of war

Understanding my mind is

body wants

and spirit Contains emptiness

intertwined into one thought

The very thoughts that can and have causes

The beating heart to slow

The aches that need to

Break free from the enslaved mind

Yes everyday health that tends to suffer

At the hands of self

Escalate your mind thoughts to alleviate

That strangle hold that many put on self

Breathe the air of evolution not

The average unseen revolution that ties

My mind

Spirituality comes from the depth of who you are

Understanding the power that lies within

Not the teaching of someone who needs to

Be finding their own

mental health starts

With eyes that stare back

at times

It requires more

but have the strength to

Get what is needed

the physical is torn down

When the mental and spiritual are not fed

The evolution of me

To feed into a hunger that can't be explained

The emotions that connect to the nerves that explode

With mystery… see what some think they understand is

Still yet to unfold before them …to let go and allow

The hormones to direct what is deeper than

Many will venture to go…

It is the ultimate release of

Control the deep that makes the clock of understanding tic

A Kiss from my perspective….signed Air

I sit and wait

contemplating what I shall witness as the sun rises

Will the desires of many hearts come to fruition?

I share in all that they do

Loving the slow, fast passionate kisses

I am the air that allows all that comes between two erotic souls

The look in her eyes

Wanting to kiss him slow and long

As he sits by and wonders what comes after the kiss

I know that look

He wants to kiss both sets of her lips

And she has not a clue

But I will be the threesome that no one knows exist

Because without me there will be nothing

As their lips come close

I feel the heat

Damn I am always the one caught in the middle

As their lips meet

Lips suffocate on me

Wet and hot

And damn the dancing their tongues do around me

But they have to come up for me

He responded just right

And his hands traveled

To feel the wettest of lips

And his lips and I traveled with him

He placed his lips upon her wet hot yoni

And she used me, with the screams that released

He kissed her lips

Sucked each one deep in between his and she used me again

Loud moans released

And he continued

He gets hotter and so do I

He continue to suck her

While his fingers penetrated her valley

She received a tongue bath with strokes

That gave me life

As she used me one last time

She screamed, I'm cumming

And he exhaled

As he drank of her juices

The kiss that I enjoy every time they share with me….

The air that they breathe…..deep rivers

"The Bare Complexity of Simplistic Love " Sweet, deep,raw, yet, a shallow explanation that speaks volumes.......

The simple but complex moment

When you realize you are slowly falling

You have no clue that this is taking place

As your life moves faster than light

And the reality is

If you slow down long enough

You would know exactly what this is

See love is more than a notion

It is deep in the wombs of who we are

To finally reach a place that no one else

Has ever been able to reach

I want this to be the love letter that only he

Will understand

No matter how many grace the words

Or even think they know

He will

And if he doesn't

Then he has no clue

That I am slowly falling

Rewind

He captured my attention

The odd catch

I believe we saw each other and silence

But all things happen for a reason

Whether it was the wrong season

Or not

It finally happened and now

To see what comes next

I don't know if he knows but I am slowly falling

I believe he is too

And if

That is

The case

I will gladly fall with him

Not many realize that the greatest love letter of all

Is simple after all

Dear XXXX,

I love you.......deep rivers

What is obvious is the focus of own, the detail of attention, the cry of desire, the burn of internal fire...........''Me, Myself, and My Needs...........Are You Ready" ?

Crippling thoughts

Crucifying images

With contorted conversations

That give misconceptions of what reality is

Fear of the unknown

Or the obvious that sits at the end of a crooked driveway

Tossed back and forth

With images that give and take life away

Baffling words that get caught on his every sound

Words that have meaning

Until they fall in an open sea

Of confusion

A temptress

Filled with nights of storms

Succulent juices

That became the glue to our souls

And that is only the beginning of what becomes

The preface of the next book

Give me what I don't have to ask for

Taste me when my well needs to be wet again

Rippling waters

With honey tips

And strawberry strokes

To read between my lines

While understanding the need

That needs to be fed

Demanding explosion after explosion

The moment when I realize

To satisfy

An addiction

That never goes away

Can he?

My appetite

Insatiable….deep rivers

To see me through your eyes
beauty you call it
and somewhere it got lost in my mind
but to see me through your eyes
I must see the eyes of he that sees me

Has he ever stopped and wondered
what that soft breeze is that caresses his cheek
randomly when least expected
or the nights that I lay awake
and yes, it is you that had my thoughts
wrapped and held tightly

To have presence without being present
as the what if floats
above troubled waters
and the thought of you brought about calm
A voice that I listened to hearing what he didn't say
but I understood

He has stimulated my mind
and stirred thoughts that even I
simply smile
I am humbly just me
and you humble as you are
carry the strength of your name

King, never used lightly and lived daily
you are the reason I smile
as I feel you deep in my soul
crossing deep waters
with passionate rivers
you are, you
and that keeps me smiling
always

"In Retrospect of My Reality "

I look back and realize so many things

I have been molested

raped

abused

and misused

and I still stand

and so many times you told me it was my fault

You always say I need to change

So as I look back

You have given me many reasons why

I need to change

You continue to tell me what I can't do

I need to change

If you insist on looking that way

Walking that way

And talking as if you don't know that you

Need to change

Mountains erect, not sideways

Waterfalls allow for the water to run down, not up

And if I choose

And yes I do have the right to choose

My glass may be half full today

And half empty tomorrow

Forward my reverse and understand it is for me to decide

Refuse my choice and that is your right to have

My success not determined by your standards

Nor is my failure sitting at your footsteps of responsibility

And through it all you continue to tell me

I need to change

You are not telling me I need to change

But the realization is that you don't want me to change for the betterment of me

You want me to fit into society…..

That just won't do…..

I am always going to be me…deep rivers

Thank you to my brother-in-law for all the amazing titles that you see in this book. I never knew how much the titles would complete some of my favorite pieces. Jaimes Monroe, thank you for each one you carefully gave each piece.

Contact me

Dawn Blanchard

deeprivers67@yahoo.com

www.ingramcontent.com/pod-product-compliance
Lightning Source LLC
Chambersburg PA
CBHW021438080526
44588CB00009B/584